A Mixed Bag

The Stuff of Life

A Mixed Bag
The Stuff of Life

Mari Jane Hillyer

Copyright © 2015 Mari Jane Hillyer

Second Edition: June 2020

All rights reserved. No part of this book may be reproduced
in any form without permission of the author,
except for brief quotations embodied in articles or reviews.

Published in the United States of America

Jadestone Books

ISBN: 978-1-930835-27-6

Library of Congress Number
2015960988

Printed on recycled, acid-free paper with non-toxic soy inks.

Manufactured in the United States of America

10 9 8 7 6 5 4 3 2

I dedicate this collection
in memory of my mother Valora

Contents

Country sea	13
The golden sea	14
The healer	15
Happy	21
One sunny day	23
Rich or poor?	24
Romance?	28
Sweet memory	29
Freedom flies	32
Morning breaks	33
River wild	34
Dream	35
Wings	37
Mr. finnigan	38
Beauty	41
Where's the gold?	42
Beautiful faces	43
Beauty two	44
Faithful glasses	45

Beauty three	47
Wiley	48
Happy two	50
Sweet song	51
Knots	52
Born in september	53
My country	55
Life anew	56

A Mixed Bag

Country sea

in the midst
of a pine tree
great beauty is found
as there is at sea

kites
high
seagulls in flight

children
in pinafores dance
not a cloud nearby

The golden sea

i think
of the lighthouse
i thought was a ship

i imagine
mom on this ship
set where sky
meets water

i imagine
those on the other side
of her
saying hi
while i
say goodbye
and the ship sails with her

The healer

a sand dollar
a gift
for i
lying
by the sea
stealing tears
away from me

i was walking along
thinking
about squiggles
in the sand
close to where water
meets land

early clammers
seagulls
the song
of the surf
a clear blue sky
strolling
along

i thought
about artistic marks
where land
meets water
i thought of how
they might have come
to be

was it the
mark of shells
washing
from sea

i was walking
along where
water meets land
and
i thought, no
there were
many and few
shells along
miles of fine sand

then i thought
maybe a picture
was drawn
by the sea

a gift to me
love,
mother sea

i looked
down at my feet
another gift given
to me
sweet
a sand dollar
perfect
unbroken
a rarity
found at my feet
where land
meets water

the song of the sea
sang her song
a gift to all
not just me
and so i continued
to stroll with my
star of the sea
unbroken
whole
a gift to me
i continued my stroll

clam diggers
chatted with gaiety
i could not help
but overhear
after all they
were so
near

i walked up
to them and they
looked at me
"are not they
beautiful
gifts of the sea?"
someone else
is thinking like me

i looked in a netted bag
admirable
they were right
simply beautiful

"i found a sand dollar"
"i found two,
let me see
i'll give one to you,"
he said to me
the clam digger
by the sea

he told me a story
not one that
everyone has heard
but one about a sand dollar
and a bird

i said mine was fuzzy
the gray sand dollar
i found by the sea

i showed it to him
the clam digger

he said, "it's alive
without water
it will not
survive"
and so i gave
my gift away
back
to the sea
from where it came
to me

i strolled away
with another gift
given to me
two white

sand dollars
stars of the sea
given to me
by the clam digger
listening
to the song
of the sea

Happy

clam diggers
are friendly people
i saw the man again
he and his son
digging
for clams
"oh i found
another
one!"
the excitement
was contagious
people of all ages

a long line
a line long
with friendly people
people friendly
standing in a
morning tide
happy
side by side
a long line
a line long
backs to me
facing mother sea

i walked in fine grains
white to the sea
and who should
i come upon again
but the clam digger
and his son
by the sea

"hi," he smiled
holding a treasure
a tiny sand dollar
delicate as could be
washed in
by the morning wave
of a welcome sea

he showed it to me
i too had one
tucked away
a tiny
sand dollar
a star of the sea
fine delicate
as could be
one gift to me
another to he
love,
mother sea

One sunny day

it is a new
day and i'm
out with
clam diggers
to play

Rich or poor?

"i'm poor."
i've heard it many
times before
from her…from him
louisa
joe
and jim
i lived among the poor
rusty was my trailer
door
was i poor
oh i am not sure
i didn't own a fancy car
or fur

but i was content
to be happy
in my normalcy
as defined
in poor peoples'
dictionary

many meanings
may claim a word
many words

may claim
a meaning

"i am poor"
i have heard it
many times before
i have lived with the poor
not very long
i must admit
did i open a
rusty trailer door
but through the years
which are many
i have worked
many a day
which to me was play
hugging
smiling
saying things
like, "you're awesome"
to asume
the black haired
little one
who was about
half of eleven
bringing a smile
to many a complacent face
"oh you did it, let's do it again!"
i would say

i would give
"the rich"
a high five
and a low one too
hugs and smiles
skies of blue
the rich i gave my heart to
in tattered blue jeans
stained tees
and a borrowed shoe

simply dear to me
asume
naturally rich
i believe happy in his normalcy
did he have new jeans
did he own a cell phone

did his daddy
own a sailboat to sail
across a golden sea
these he did not
need
he is rich
because he is happy

now when i hear
"i am poor"
i wonder
does it mean
more?

Romance?

romance
vanilla seeds
no it's not
for me
i am a male
a street sweeper
who rides
a tortoise to sea
my favorite place
to be
waves sweeping
over me
sand sticking
on my feet
high tide asking
me to play
i'm a streetsweeping male
on vacation
today

Sweet memory

home to me
is many things
a long driveway
a cottonwood tree
a place to be
with mom always
there with a homemade
brownie
with a marshmallow swirl
or a steaming
pot roast
mashed potatoes
gravy
the aroma
of which i long for
a memory

home to me
is many things
a place of lakes
rivers and streams
a mountain view
of amazing blue
hue which only dreams
are made of

cornfields
plains
sunsets spread across
horizons wide
family
friends

home to me
is many things
many homes have i
soon i will go home
to one of my
homes
its walls will look the same
no apple pie
the couch will be
in the same place
and the well-worn stools
will stand by the old counter top
and i will gaze at curtains of cream lace

home as i have known it
since i can remember
will no longer be
it will be empty of the one
who made it
home for
me

my home is a building
now filled
with the aroma of fresh
memories
pot roast
mashed potatoes
gravy
and the one
who made them
for me

Freedom flies

a wisp of wind
cools
i sit streetside
the curb feels
rough to me
i am thankful
for freedom
a fighter jet
is music to me
i hear freedom
singing its
melody
much like the
roar of a
rushing sea
the red white and blue
as beautiful as an
imperfect world
can be
my country

Morning breaks

a
deer came today
fuzzy antlers
young at play
nibbling

a
weedy green
by a juniper
tree

a
northern flicker
came today
mr. bob
or
mrs. maybe
soon i see
three
kings
of the suet
by a
juniper tree

River wild

river
sing me your song
water
carry me on
to where one knows
carry me on to the sea

it is where it goes
oh carry me on
i need the river's song
carry me on
oh river
sing me your
song

Dream

well well
what do you do
if you don't
dream up
a story
or a nostalgic
piece of poetry

what do you do
when your mind is free
if you are an artist
you may close your eyes
and see
the sea
pick up your brush
and paint
the scene

if you are a musician
you may pick up your mandolin
play a song
for me
or imagine a picture in words
some soft melody

maybe about a rose
a rose thorn free

i cannot speak for you
but for me
i love the song
of the sea
and so each day i create

rushing waves
sand beneath my feet
a river running
free
a babbling brook
the song of the sea

Wings

two
stellar jays
hang at my
birdfeeder
today
one wants
to eat
the other
play

Mr. finnigan

oh mr. finnigan
why don't you
begin again

fifty quail
waddle by
i hear
the jay cry

oh mr. finnigan
why don't you
live again

the city
wakes up
he stares
with his coffee cup

caught
in a web tangle
refusing to unmangle

in his own prison
is he refusing

to break out
be free

oh mr. finnigan
why don't you
begin again
oh
mr. finnigan
why don't you
begin to live again

there's a future ahead
of you
i see it
skys of blue
oh mr. finnigan
why can't you

oh mr. finnigan
live again
please
remember it's never
to late
to become
what you might
have been

so please try
mr. finnigan
oh
live again
live again
become what
you might have been

oh
live again
live again
please
mr. finnigan

Beauty

one fuzzy antlered
deer came yesterday
peered into my window
like he wanted to play
still as could be
a statue
when he saw
me shooting
with my cannon
click
click
click

i shot a fuzzy
antlered deer today

Where's the gold?

i'm tired
of chasing rainbows

Beautiful faces

i love
to be among
poor people
torn tees
old tennies
maybe no front
teeth
i love to be
among the poor
the needy
walmart
i am
at

Beauty two

the deer
washed each other
with delight
as i went

click
click
click

through the screen door

Faithful glasses

wiping tears away
a rose filled
hanky
old fashioned
delicate
so pretty

the silver hair
of a lady
sitting there
the gentle wave
the color they shared
i saw my mother
oh so pretty

dressed like a million dollars
slight bigger than my mother
the lady
sitting there
so much in style
they shared

i looked at the pew
in front of her and there

sat another
a lady
oh so fair
silver was her hair
more curly
petite
her size
looked familiar

my rose hanky
oh so pretty
used on a sun filled day

i slipped on vintage glasses
striped black and white
not that i
needed to shield the light

Beauty three

jays caw
a tiger stripe
purrs
coffee drips
morning breaks
it is tomorrow

Wiley

she looked at me
"are you from
virginia?"
i stepped out
of an old suv
i looked up and saw
a tall lady
missing front teeth
"well i was" i told her
"it is my son's car"
and that he had
driven oh so far
we chatted
about sunsets
spread across a wide sky
she asked if we liked it here
"it's beautiful" said i

i smiled at her
a face of the poor living
in a broken down rv
beautiful
was she
a tall lady
nothing fancy

simple clothes
a face of the poor
i like the poor
i like
walmart
i like
wiley
outside
a post office
door
the last thing
she said to me
was "i didn't know
if you would talk to me"
"it is a pleasure"

i smiled at her
a face of the poor
many meanings claim
a word
many words claim
a meaning
does poor
mean something
more
maybe–
happy in her
normalcy
wiley

Happy two

if we all
liked everyone
what a different
place
our world
would be
no more fighting

no war
peace
love
joy
on a distant
shore
what a different
place
our world
would be
come dream with me

Sweet song

robins
year around
i do not know
why they are found
in the mountain air
where the wind doesn't
blow
they are just there
that's all
i know

Knots

knots
knots
plain knots
old
knots
and then there are
knots
not
just knots
but knots
of pain

Born in september

i always
thought it would be nice
to have a little desk
with a mountain
view to write by
i have it now
surreal blue

i always
thought it would be nice
to have a mother's ring
with five stones
i have one now

a mother's ring
with diamonds
and more

one birthstone
a star sapphire
my mother's ring
did she have it
made for me

someday i will know
when I get to the place
where the rivers run free

i always thought
it would be nice
to have a slice
of heaven

My country

i see freedom staring at me
the red white and blue
still as can be
the world
open and wide

through a glass window
pane i see
a pine tree
in spring breeze

where is the sun–
is it playing
peek a boo
with me?

Life anew

you're starting
to live again
thank you mr. finnigan

the end
or maybe
the beginning

www.ingramcontent.com/pod-product-compliance
Lightning Source LLC
Chambersburg PA
CBHW050841040426
42333CB00058B/385